THIS PAGE:
View of Grant-Kohrs Ranch NHS, MT

ON THE COVER:
Scenic vista of the ranch at Grant-Kohrs Ranch NHS, MT

NPS Photos

Grant- Kohrs Ranch National Historic Site

Geologic Resource Evaluation Report

Natural Resource Report NPS/NRPC/GRD/NRR—2007/004

Geologic Resources Division
Natural Resource Program Center
P.O. Box 25287
Denver, Colorado 80225

June 2007

U.S. Department of the Interior
Washington, D.C.

The Natural Resource Publication series addresses natural resource topics that are of interest and applicability to a broad readership in the National Park Service and to others in the management of natural resources, including the scientific community, the public, and the NPS conservation and environmental constituencies. Manuscripts are peer-reviewed to ensure that the information is scientifically credible, technically accurate, appropriately written for the intended audience, and is designed and published in a professional manner.

Natural Resource Reports are the designated medium for disseminating high priority, current natural resource management information with managerial application. The series targets a general, diverse audience, and may contain NPS policy considerations or address sensitive issues of management applicability. Examples of the diverse array of reports published in this series include vital signs monitoring plans; "how to" resource management papers; proceedings of resource management workshops or conferences; annual reports of resource programs or divisions of the Natural Resource Program Center; resource action plans; fact sheets; and regularly-published newsletters.

Views and conclusions in this report are those of the authors and do not necessarily reflect policies of the National Park Service. Mention of trade names or commercial products does not constitute endorsement or recommendation for use by the National Park Service.

Printed copies of reports in these series may be produced in a limited quantity and they are only available as long as the supply lasts. This report is also available from the Geologic Resource Evaluation Program website (http://www2.nature.nps.gov/geology/inventory/gre_publications) on the internet, or by sending a request to the address on the back cover. Please cite this publication as:

Thornberry-Ehrlich, T. 2007. Grant-Kohrs Ranch National Historic Site Geologic Resource Evaluation Report. Natural Resource Report NPS/NRPC/GRD/NRR—2007/004. National Park Service, Denver, Colorado.

NPS D-58, June 2007

Table of Contents

List of Figures

Executive Summary

This report has been developed to accompany the digital geologic map produced by Geologic Resource Evaluation staff for Grant- Kohrs Ranch National Historic Site in Montana. It contains information relevant to resource management and scientific research.

Grant- Kohrs Ranch National Historic Site commemorates the western ranch lifestyle as part of a living museum. Simultaneously, the park protects a portion of the upper Clark Fork River drainage. Grant- Kohrs Ranch lies within the Northern Rocky Mountains Physiographic Province, which contains metamorphic, sedimentary, and igneous rocks of Precambrian to Tertiary age as well as recent alluvial and glacial deposits. The pre- Tertiary rocks are complex and were folded and deformed multiple times during the Sevier and Laramide orogenic events.

Underlying geologic structure, past and present, defines every natural landscape. Geologic processes give rise to rock formations, mountains and valleys, mineral deposits, and broad river plains. The results of these processes played a prominent role in the history of the Clark Fork River Valley with regard to both mining activity and cattle ranching. Understanding Grant- Kohrs Ranch begins with the geology and with the processes from which today's environments, history, and scenery arose.

Geologic processes develop a landscape that influences human use patterns. The geology inspires wonder in visitors to Grant- Kohrs Ranch, and emphasizing it enhances the visitor experience. Rich geological, historical, and cultural resources impact land- use and visitor use planning in the park. Adding a detailed geologic map, wayside exhibits, a road or trail log, and a guidebook that ties Grant- Kohrs Ranch to the other parks in the Northern Rocky Mountains, and to the park's existing portfolio of visitor information would enhance visitor appreciation of the geologic history and dynamic processes that created the natural landscape and could emphasize the long history showcased at the park.

Humans have significantly modified the landscape and the geologic system surrounding Grant- Kohrs Ranch through mining and agriculture. Wastes from mining and smelting threaten ecosystem health, which is capable of noticeable change within a human life span. Acid mine drainage and heavy metal contamination are serious resource management concerns for Grant- Kohrs Ranch.

The Clark Fork River is the lifeline of the vast Deer Lodge Valley. Intense seasonal precipitation and high runoff cause flooding along the upper reaches of the Clark Fork River. Grant- Kohrs Ranch is located downstream of many former mining operations in the upper Clark Fork River Drainage. Abandoned and inactive mines pose a threat to health, safety, and the environmental in the Grant- Kohrs Ranch area.

Foremost among these is metal contamination of groundwater, surface water, and soils. Metal- rich flood-plain deposits, derived from contaminated sediments dispersed during floods in the late 1800's- early 1900's, flank the Clark Fork River. The quality of the surface water system is threatened by the continuous re-exposure to heavy metals eroded from floodplain deposits. Due to mining related contamination the Environmental Protection Agency (EPA) has designated the upper Clark Fork River as a superfund site.

Erosion along the riverbanks in the area increases the overall sediment carried by the park's streams and exposes aquatic ecosystems to further contamination once trapped in sediments. Heavy metal levels are elevated in the Clark Fork River sediments. Even changes in relatively clean sediment loads and distribution affect aquatic and riparian ecosystems. Sediment loading can change channel morphology and increase overbank- flooding frequency.

The Clark Fork River with its associated hydrogeologic system is a primary resource at the park. Most working aquifers are at shallow levels in unconsolidated Quaternary and Tertiary deposits. Groundwater inflow is an important contributor to the water budget of the river in the park area. A working model of the hydrogeologic system within the park is needed to predict environmental responses to contaminants and to help remediate affected areas.

Introduction

The following section briefly describes the regional geologic setting and the National Park Service Geologic Resource Evaluation program.

Purpose of the Geologic Resource Evaluation Program

The Geologic Resource Evaluation (GRE) Program is one of 12 inventories funded under the NPS Natural Resource Challenge designed to enhance baseline information available to park managers. The program carries out the geologic component of the inventory effort from the development of digital geologic maps to providing park staff with a geologic report tailored to a park's specific geologic resource issues. The Geologic Resources Division of the Natural Resource Program Center administers this program. The GRE team relies heavily on partnerships with the U.S. Geological Survey, Colorado State University, state surveys, and others in developing GRE products.

The goal of the GRE Program is to increase understanding of the geologic processes at work in parks and provide sound geologic information for use in park decision making. Sound park stewardship relies on understanding natural resources and their role in the ecosystem. Geology is the foundation of park ecosystems. The compilation and use of natural resource information by park managers is called for in section 204 of the National Parks Omnibus Management Act of 1998 and in NPS- 75, Natural Resources Inventory and Monitoring Guideline.

To realize this goal, the GRE team is systematically working towards providing each of the identified 270 natural area parks with a geologic scoping meeting, a digital geologic map, and a geologic report. During scoping meetings the GRE team brings together park staff and geologic experts to review available geologic maps and discuss specific geologic issues, features, and processes. Scoping meetings are usually held for individual parks and on occasion for an entire Vital Signs Monitoring Network. The GRE mapping team converts the geologic maps identified for park use at the scoping meeting into digital geologic data in accordance with their innovative Geographic Information Systems (GIS) Data Model. These digital data sets bring an exciting interactive dimension to traditional paper maps by providing geologic data for use in park GIS and facilitating the incorporation of geologic considerations into a wide range of resource management applications. The newest maps come complete with interactive help files. As a companion to the digital geologic maps, the GRE team prepares a park- specific geologic report that aids in use of the maps and provides park managers with an overview of park geology and geologic resource management issues.

For additional information regarding the content of this report and up to date GRE contact information please refer to the Geologic Resource Evaluation web site (http://www2.nature.nps.gov/geology/inventory/).

Geologic Setting

Grant- Kohrs Ranch once encompassed 10 million acres of a cattle empire near Deer Lodge, Montana. Today this 1,618- acre site is the only unit in the National Park Service commemorating the frontier ranch lifestyle. The historic site was designated an NPS unit on March 30, 1971, and authorized August 25, 1972. John Francis Grant first developed the ranch in 1862. Grant sold the ranch to Conrad Kohrs in 1866. Kohrs expanded the ranch, taking advantage of the free range in western Montana. Today, the site contains 90 historic structures and maintains active cattle ranch operations in the Deer Lodge Valley. This living museum attracts 15,000+ visitors annually.

Grant- Kohrs Ranch National Historic Site sits in the broad Deer Lodge Valley of the Clark Fork River in west- central Montana (figure 1). The valley includes approximately 775 square kilometers (300 square miles) in Powell, Deer Lodge, and Silver Bow counties (Konizeski et al. 1968). The headwaters of the Clark Fork River are located south of Grant- Kohrs Ranch where the Silver Bow and Warm Springs creeks merge. Structurally this valley is a half graben bounded on the western edge by normal faults at the range front. Mountains in this area include the Flint Creek, Anaconda, and Highland ranges. The eastern side of the Deer Lodge Valley lacks distinct fault boundaries, but is ultimately defined by the Boulder Mountains and further north, the Garnet Mountains. Mt. Haggin (3,250 m, 10,665 ft above sea level) is the highest point within the upper Clark Fork drainage area. These ranges are all part of the Northern Rocky Mountains physiographic province characterized by rugged mountains and intermontane valleys.

Local geology varies greatly within the Grant- Kohrs Ranch area. In the eastern mountains, the Cretaceous Boulder Batholith granitic (monzogranite, granodiorite, and aplite) igneous intrusion is the predominant rock type. Several high- angle normal faults cut the area trending north, northwest, and northeast. Along the western side of the valley, the rocks are comprised of folded and faulted sedimentary units intruded by Cretaceous granitic to dioritic igneous dikes and stocks. Vast mineral deposits in the 16 different mining districts of the area are a result of this igneous activity (Madison et al. 1998). The upper Clark Fork River is the primary waterway in the area. Its basin covers more than 3,370 square km (1,300 square miles). Local tributaries and small streams include Tin Cup Joe, Fred Burr, Cottonwood, Peterson, and Dempsey creeks (Nimick 1993). Thick deposits of alluvium form terraces and rolling hills along the valley (Konizeski et al. 1968).

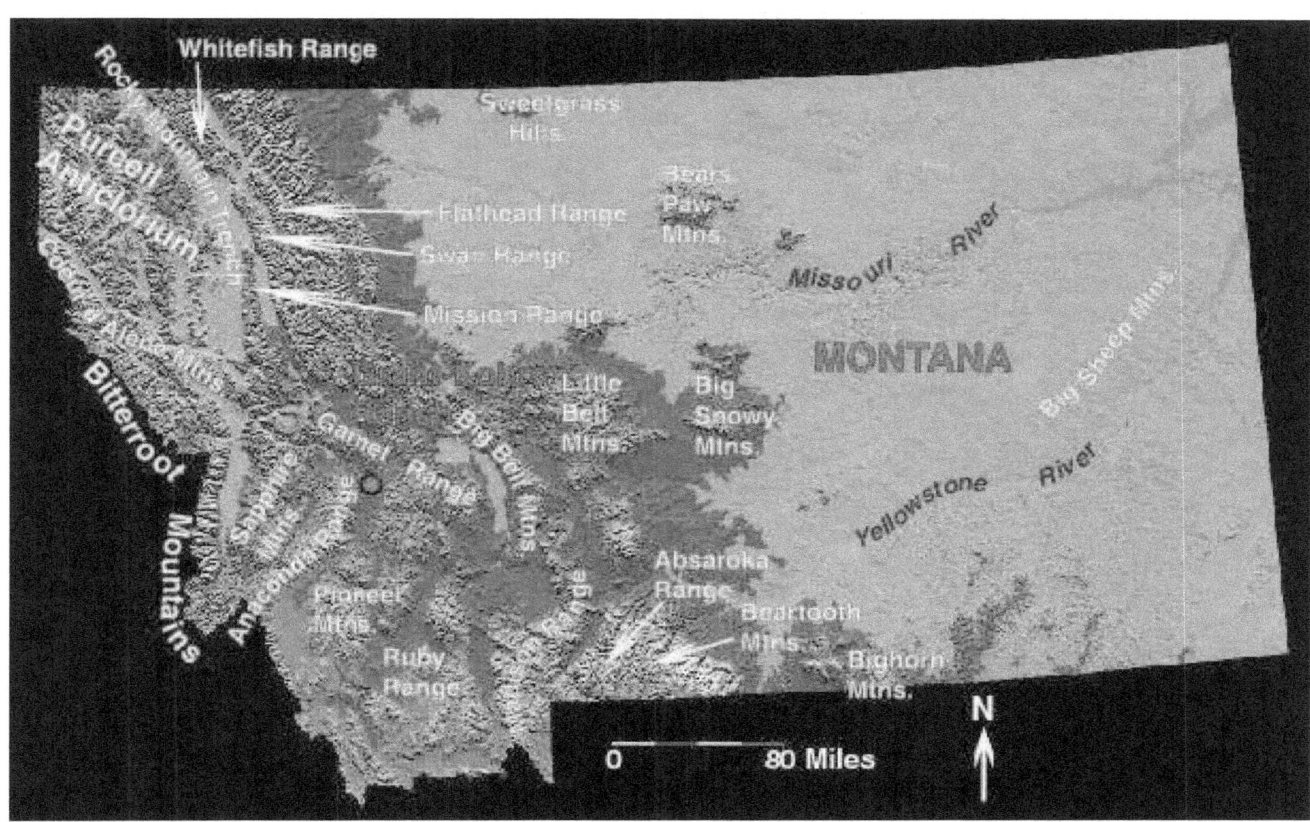

Figure 1. Map of Montana with physiographic features surrounding Grant-Kohrs Ranch National Historic Site. Modified version of map from Perry-Castañeda Library Map Collection.

Geologic Issues

A Geologic Resource Evaluation scoping session was held for Grant-Kohrs Ranch National Historic Site on August 19, 2002, to discuss geologic resources, address the status of geologic mapping, and assess resource management issues and needs. The following section synthesizes the scoping results, in particular, those issues that may require attention from resource managers.

Introduction

Recent human activity in the area has had some dramatic effects on the landscape. Early mining efforts released tailings and waste into the system. In addition, overgrazing by cattle (reducing the riparian buffer zone) has caused massive erosion. The combined result was the deposition of extensive floodplain deposits contaminated with heavy metals. Since the early 1900s, sediment management systems on the Clark Fork River and tributaries have lessened flooding, but regular stream migration and seasonal high flows are reworking contaminated sediments, reintroducing them to the environment at Grant-Kohrs Ranch National Historic Site (Nimick 1990).

Geologic issues in this section are centered around historic mining issues with sub-categories relating primarily to that major issue. Potential research projects and topics of scientific interest are also presented at the end of the section.

Historic Mining Issues

Mining is not allowed in the park under existing federal law; however, the legacy of past mining in the area continues to affect the resources of Grant-Kohrs Ranch National Historic Site. According to the reclamation summary of abandoned mineral lands in the National Park Service conducted by the Disturbed Lands Restoration Program of the Geologic Resources Division, there is an abandoned mine feature at Grant-Kohrs Ranch. There are many more mine-related features beyond park boundaries. Abandoned and inactive mines create safety, environmental, and health concerns for the Grant-Kohrs Ranch area. Foremost among these is metal contamination of groundwater, surface water, and soils. Contamination is defined as the occurrence of metals exceeding baseline concentrations. Baseline concentrations are the probable concentration levels prior to mining activities (Moore and Woessner 2000). In addition to water and soil contamination, air pollution results when dust blows from abandoned tailing piles. Further, tailing and other mill waste piles as well as mine openings and dilapidated structures have the potential for collapse and pose serious safety hazards (Madison et al. 1998).

Metal concentrations in water, sediment, soils, and biota in the area are elevated due to historic mining practices, smelting, and natural mineralization (Smith et al. 1998). Between 1878 and 1925, over ten million tons of waste produced from smelting and milling activity in Butte alone were disposed of in Silver Bow Creek, near the headwaters of the Clark Fork River (Nimick 1990).

Grant-Kohrs Ranch is located downstream from many mine operations in the upper Clark Fork River Drainage. Metal-rich flood-plain deposits flank the river from Warm Springs to Milltown Reservoir near Missoula, Montana (Smith et al. 1998). Due to the presence of hazardous substances related to mining activity throughout the region, the U.S. Environmental Protection Agency (EPA) designated the upper Clark Fork River as a superfund site, an operative unit of the Milltown Reservoir Superfund Site (Breuninger 2000). According to the historic site's annual report for FY05, ongoing projects to install monitoring wells and lined irrigation ditches are a priority at Grant-Kohrs Ranch National Historic Site and financial negotiations between the Federal Government and responsible parties for superfund issues are still in progress (Rotegard 2006). The Montana Bureau of Mines and Geology (MBMG) and the U.S. Forest Service (USFS) studied this area regarding potential problems associated with abandoned and inactive mines. For the park, the study found that the potential for acid mine drainage is a serious resource management concern.

Acid mine drainage is a condition resulting from sulfides reacting with water and lowering the pH by producing sulfuric acid (H_2SO_4), sulfate (SO_4^{2-}), and reduced iron (Fe^{2+}). This acidity increases the solubility of some potentially harmful metals. These metals are then dispersed from a mine source area by ground and surface water as dissolved ions, suspended sediment, or as part of the fluvial bedload (Madison et al. 1998).

There are at least six components dictating the formation of acid mine drainage conditions (Trexler et al. 1975):

1. availability of sulfides (including pyrite),
2. presence of oxygen and iron-oxidizing bacteria,
3. water in the atmosphere,
4. availability of metals and minerals,
5. availability of water to transport dissolved components, and
6. mine and waste area characteristics.

These components, present in mined areas upstream from Grant-Kohrs Ranch, have produced acid mine drainage. Once formed, the acidic water dissolves other minerals including sulfides such as arsenopyrite, chalcopyrite, tetrahedrite, galena, and sphalerite as well as aluminosilicate minerals.

Metals such as manganese, silver, arsenic, copper, aluminum, cadmium, mercury, lead, zinc, and iron are present in the water as cations. When cation concentrations are high enough and pH rises (higher than 2.2) due to dilution, minerals containing these dissolved metals begin to precipitate ferric hydroxide $(Fe[OH]_3)$ and other insoluble metal compounds (Madison et al. 1998; Schlumberger 2007). Precipitates cloud surface water, coat rocks, and deposit in layers in floodplain areas and along streambeds.

Within the upper Clark Fork River drainage area, the MBMG and USFS study investigated 179 abandoned-inactive mines and/or mills for potential environmental impacts. Many of these sites are upstream from Grant-Kohrs Ranch and may affect water and sediment quality within the park. These areas ranged from small hillslope prospects and adits to larger underground systems. Tailings from these mines have been, and continue to be, eroded, mixed with other sediments, transported downstream, and deposited in stream channels and floodplains as a result of fluvial processes such as a flattening of the gradient (Dodge et al. 2004). Because Grant-Kohrs Ranch sits in the downstream reaches of the upper Clark Fork River drainage (drainage area of 2,600 square km, 1,005 square miles), environmental impacts from these upstream mines and tailings are a serious management concern (Madison et al. 1998).

One of the closest mines to the ranch is the Champion mine and the accompanying mill about 19 km (12 miles) southeast of the town of Deer Lodge, Montana. The Dark Horse Mill sits west of the town of Racetrack, near Deer Lodge. The Ding Bat and Blue Eyed Maggie mines are 11 km (7 miles) east of Deer Lodge and Grant-Kohrs Ranch. Also nearby, are the Lower Hidden Hand, Racetrack, Sterrit, St Mary, and Rock Gulch mines.

The Champion, Lower Hidden Hand, Racetrack, St. Mary, Sterrit, and Ding Bat mines show high levels of mercury in water tested by the MBMG and USFS study. Arsenic is concentrated in water at Ding Bat and Rocker Gulch mines; manganese is concentrated at Lower Hidden Hand mine; and lead, chlorine, and silver are concentrated in the water at Racetrack mine (Madison et al. 1998).

Trace elements derived from mining, smelting, and milling activities in the area over the past 135 years (Nimick 1993), have contaminated broad land areas along the upper Clark Fork River drainage. Erosion of tailings deposits in the flood-plain is a major contributor of metals to the watershed (Smith et al. 1998). Elements of specific concern include arsenic, cadmium, copper, iron, lead, manganese, and zinc. Soil studies revealed high levels of arsenic, cadmium, copper, lead, and zinc at several mines upstream of Grant-Kohrs Ranch (Madison et al. 1998). Arsenic and cadmium have been

identified in elevated concentrations in local groundwater supplies (Nimick 1993).

Because continuous erosion of floodplain deposits and riverbanks redistributes (and slightly dilutes) heavy metals, the ecosystem is constantly re-exposed to contamination (Breuninger 2000). In situ remediation efforts to restore stable, healthy conditions within selected areas of the watershed such as the South Deer Lodge Improvement Project, the Governor's Demonstration Project, and the Warm Springs Pond/Mill Willow Bypass cleanup showed no significant change to basin scale contaminant levels in 7 years between 1991 and 1998 (Breuninger 2000).

Heavy metal contamination may impose chronic toxicity on biota of the upper Clark Fork River basin. In the reach of the river near Grant-Kohrs Ranch, flood-plain deposits and exposed tailing piles are extensive, as much as 0.3 m (1 ft) thick on terraces 2 m (6 ft) above the river (Nimick 1990; Smith et al. 1998; Breuninger 2000). Floodplain sediments are enriched in heavy metals as much as 1,800 times over background (Nimick 1990). Waste trapped in higher areas spread over the Clark Fork River valley during at least four large floods in the late 1800's and early 1900's (Nimick 1990). Within local valley fill, an arsenic-rich flood deposit stands out as a yellow layer (Bruce Heise, personal communication 2005). Resource management needs to understand the nature of these potential threats to the ecosystem health.

The toxicity of heavy metals is manifested by disrupting cellular enzymes, which run on nutritional minerals such as magnesium, zinc, and selenium. Heavy metals replace the nutrients and bind their receptor sites, causing diffuse symptoms by affecting nerves, hormones, digestion, and immune function. Threats to plant communities include loss in biodiversity, and toxicity, whereas in fish and aquatic life, toxicity and bioaccumulation threatens predatory species that consume them. In humans, heavy metal toxicity leads to myriad health problems ranging from memory loss, increased allergic reactions, high blood pressure, depression, mood swings, irritability, poor concentration, aggressive behavior, sleep disabilities, fatigue, speech disorders, high blood pressure, cholesterol, triglycerides, vascular occlusion, neuropathy, autoimmune diseases, and chronic fatigue (I.H. 2007).

To better understand mining impacts and contamination transport processes, Grant-Kohrs Ranch National Historic Site had an in-depth environmental quality assessment done in cooperation with several universities. It is entitled "US Department of Interior Site Characterization and Natural Resource Damage Assessment Studies, Grant-Kohrs Ranch NHS and Bureau of Land Management, 2000-2001; Clark Fork River Operable Unit of the Milltown Reservoir Sediments NPL Site; July 8, 2002". Other recent works by the Department of the Interior related to the Superfund site of the Clark Fork River Valley, including soil and groundwater contamination studies, are available through the department.

Geology and Biology

Geology forms the basis of the ecosystem at Grant-Kohrs Ranch National Historic Site. Watersheds containing abandoned and inactive mines are continually at risk of heavy metal contamination through the processes of waste rock leaching, groundwater flow, redistribution of tailings, and particulate air-fall (Breuninger 2000; Butler 2003).

Metals contained in riverine sediments are linked to decreases in the biodiversity of the associated ecosystems (Breuninger 2000). Heavy metal bearing minerals are often altered by mining, weathering, and fluvial processes in such a way that they become more bioavailable (Nimick 1990). The effect is stair step in nature with algae and other microorganisms incorporating the metals from the environment into their structures. Fish, such as trout and other aquatic life, feed on these organisms concentrating the contaminants. Birds and mammals, such as mink and otters, eventually feed on the toxic fish (Nimick 1990; Breuninger 2000). As mentioned above, heavy metals interrupt natural cellular processes in the body and cause myriad health problems, especially concerning the nervous system (I.H. 2007).

As part of the historic site's cattle herd management strategy, controlled stretches of the Clark Fork River stream bank are fenced to prevent cattle from overgrazing delicate and threatened riparian zones. The historic site has no control over what grazing practices are adopted by neighboring private landowners. Fenced reaches barring cattle from stream banks are shown to have better fish habitat and lower overall concentrations of heavy metals (Nimick 1990).

Ongoing studies between 1993 and 2001 to determine if grazing affects biodiversity suggest plant community recovery is controlled by myriad factors beyond cattle grazing although degradations in stream bank stability were directly correlative with grazing areas (Bedunah and Jones 2001). In a study sampling riparian wetland species (e.g. cattails, *Typha latifolia*), elevated concentrations of copper, zinc, and lead were found in plant and root tissues (John 1994), in concentrations that could pose a health threat to grazing animals and in turn pose a threat to humans consuming meat or dairy from these cows.

Surface Water Movement

The upper Clark Fork River watershed covers approximately 3,370 square km (1,300 square miles). The downstream boundary of the upper Clark Fork is near the town of Drummond, Montana approximately 40 km (25 miles) northwest of Grant-Kohrs Ranch. The Clark Fork has a cobble-armored riverbed and in the Deer Lodge Valley, the river meanders through the unconsolidated valley fill from cut banks to point bars, constantly reworking the valley fill materials (figure 2) (Smith et al. 1998).

Understanding the dynamics behind surface water movement in the area is essential for resource management since the transport of heavy metals and contaminants is controlled by the supply and input rates of the material, the association between metals and the sediment, and the downstream transport of water and sediment especially during peak flow (Smith et al. 1998).

The average annual precipitation for the upper Clark Fork River ranges from 25 to 36 cm (10 to 14 inches) in the valleys to over 150 cm (60 inches) in the mountainous areas. Most of this precipitation occurs in late winter and early spring (Madison et al. 1998). Intense seasonal precipitation and/or high runoff events cause flooding along the upper Clark Fork River. Recent large mainstream peak flows occurred in 1908, 1948, 1964, 1975, 1981 with the first being the largest recorded flood event. At Deer Lodge the peak discharge for a 100-year flood is 170 m³/sec (5,900 ft³/sec).

Sediment Load and Channel Storage

Massive amounts of contaminated sediment covers the Deer Lodge Valley floor. As much as 704,000 m³ (24,862,000 ft³) of mine wastes are spread over 274 hectares along a 10 km (6 miles) stretch of the river. As these sediments are transported back and forth between the river and floodplain, there is continual re-exposure and release of toxic metals to the environment (Nimick 1990; Nimick and Moore 1994).

Erosion of the landscape within the upper Clark Fork River watershed leads to increases in sediment carried by area streams. Bank erosion is a major factor leading to the introduction of heavy metals to the riverine environment. Land use appears to affect streambank erosion rates. Cattle grazing reduces the amount of buffering and stabilizing vegetation in the riparian zones along rivers and streams. Changes in sediment loads and distribution affect aquatic and riparian ecosystems, and sediment loading can result in changes to channel morphology and increase the frequency of overbank flooding.

Elevated suspended sediment load is a resource management concern because it can contaminate drinking water sources and increase concentrations of toxic chemicals, including heavy metals and pesticides, formerly trapped in river bottom sediments. However, fine-grained sediments are also vital in the overall fluvial transport of contaminants in a water system. Thus, sediments act as contaminant sources and sinks (Breuninger 2000).

Understanding the processes involved in sediment transport is vital for evaluating the movement of heavy metals attached to sediment particles. In the Clark Fork River, sediments are transported as bedload, rolling along the gravel streambed, or in suspension, as part of the water column (Smith et al. 1998). The amount of material moved by the river depends on flow conditions and overall hydrologic energy. During seasonal high flows, the river probably transports pebble and gravel size particles as bedload and sand and finer grained particles in suspension (Smith et al. 1998). These materials are typically deposited on downstream point bars.

Channel storage of fine sediment and the contaminants contained therein follow a seasonal cycle. This cycle is subject to hydrologic variability with increased availability during the high flows of spring and decreased availability during the low flows of autumn.

Fine- grained sediments do not travel downstream in a single pulse but are often resuspended bottom material (Miller et al. 1984). This intermittent transport of contaminants and fine- grained sediment increases the affected area. Heavy metals eroded from cut banks are transported in equilibrium with other sediments, mixed at point bars. The entire process results in a continuous downstream flux of metals (Smith et al. 1998).

Groundwater Movement

The broad Deer Lodge Valley of the upper Clark Fork River drainage is floored with thick Quaternary alluvium and glacial deposits, and unconsolidated Tertiary deposits. These mixed units in the Grant- Kohrs Ranch area have developed a number of shallow water aquifers. Groundwater flow responds to variations in seasonal precipitation and is drawn from upland areas around the baseline of the Clark Fork River (Nimick 1993). Groundwater flow generally follows the topographic surface, typically flowing towards the nearest stream or river. Fractured bedrock supplies some water to the system locally.

The rate of groundwater inflow to the Clark Fork at 2.5m³/sec. (88 ft³/sec.) is significant between Racetrack and Garrison, Montana. This stretch corresponds with the location of Grant- Kohrs Ranch. Irrigation- return flow is likely responsible for this rate of inflow. Groundwater levels are highest during spring runoff and are highly influenced by local irrigation practices (Nimick 1993).

Aquifers in Quaternary alluvium yield more water to wells than those in Tertiary deposits or fractured bedrock. Quaternary alluvium and Tertiary deposits are presumably connected hydraulically, thus some groundwater flows vertically downward from the alluvium into the older deposits (Nimick 1993). Depending on slope and hydraulic gradient, groundwater is thought to move laterally through adjacent aquifers as well.

Tertiary units may be as much as 1,525 m (5,000 ft) thick beneath some reaches of the valley floor. Coarser- grained beds and lenses composed of sands and gravels develop permeable and productive aquifers. Finer- grained beds of clay and silt sized particles do not develop groundwater yielding aquifers. Due to over irrigation with unlined ditches, sprinklers, and flood systems, water levels in these deeper aquifers are generally highest in the summer months.

If the Tertiary deposits are part of a terrace structure, they typically discharge toward adjacent stream valleys into alluvium (Nimick 1993).

Bedrock aquifers (primarily in Cretaceous sedimentary units) are water sources for human use when shallow alluvium and Tertiary deposit aquifers are unavailable, usually near the valley margins. The bedrock aquifers are productive enough for domestic use, however, these are not considered a significant water source for the park. Inflow to these aquifers is generally from precipitation. Discharge points include seeps, springs, other aquifers, and streams (Nimick 1993). Spring locations are generally associated with geologic structure, mostly occurring near faults and folds associated with the valley margins.

Inventory, Monitoring, and Research Needs for Historic Mining Issues

- Determine how contaminants are transported from upstream acid mine drainage.
- Monitor biota (e.g., aquatic insects) for heavy metal contamination.
- Use pH of saturation extracts of surface samples as a pollution index to map problem areas for spot remediation, providing a short- term solution to local contamination problems (Nimick 1990).
- Spatially determine areas of non- point source runoff and study how this is affecting neighbors and the plant communities of the park.
- Determine how surface water movement is affected by surficial deposits and soils.
- Monitor discharge, pH, specific conductance, temperature, dissolved oxygen, and concentrations of cadmium, chromium, copper, lead, zinc, arsenic, iron, manganese, sulfate, and aluminum in surface waters (Duaime and Appleman 1990).
- Monitor streamflow and timing and magnitude of storm events; supplement data from fixed river- level gauges with field data on submergence and exposure of key sites that can be correlated with ecosystem response to floods and droughts.
- Investigate paleoflood hydrology.
- Conduct hydrologic condition assessments to identify actual and potential "problem reaches" (near roadways, trails, and visitor and administrative facilities) for prioritized monitoring.
- Increase monitoring of fine- sediment load in rivers and local tributaries affecting the park.
- Relate surface water movement and surficial deposits to contaminant transport.
- Measure morphologic change in stream channels related to sediment load. Reliable measurements generally require 3- 5 cross sections over several hundred meters of channel.
- Promote cattle- free riparian zones along the river corridor to reduce streambank erosion of contaminated deposits.

- Use shallow (10-inch) and deeper core data to monitor rates of sediment accumulation and erosion and analyze changes in chemical constituents of sediments.
- Cooperate with local agencies to determine amounts, types, and durations of exposure of the watershed to contaminants.
- Correlate watershed disturbance with sediment load in streams and any aquatic biological productivity reductions.
- Define the influences of bedrock and topography on local watersheds at Grant-Kohrs Ranch.

- Map and quantify water subterranean recharge zones.
- Install monitoring stations to measure atmospheric inputs of important chemical components (such as nitrogen, mercury, and pH), and outputs to groundwater.
- Investigate additional methods to characterize groundwater recharge areas and flow directions

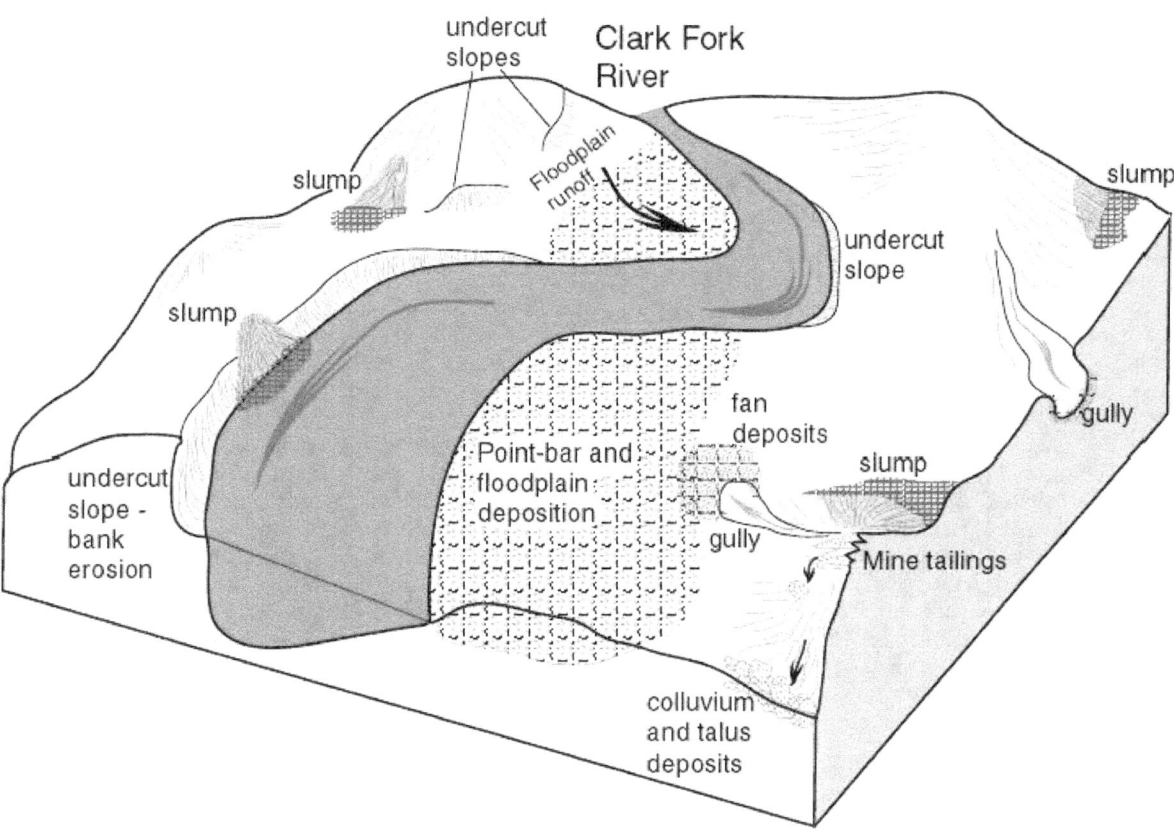

Figure 2. Diagram of stream processes on the landscape at Grant-Kohrs Ranch National Historic Site. Note the inputs of floodplain runoff and bank erosion to the sediment load of the river. Note also the deposition of deposits in point bars and floodplains. Graphic by Trista L. Thornberry-Ehrlich (Colorado State University).

Geologic Features and Processes

This section provides descriptions of the most prominent and distinctive geologic features and processes in Grant- Kohrs Ranch National Historic Site.

Geology and history connections

John Francis Grant came to the Deer Lodge Valley in 1855 to take advantage of its rolling hills for pasture, a clean river, and open spaces. Seasonal water shortages made the landscape unattractive for intensive farming; however, cattle ranching flourished (Konizeski et al. 1968).

Early mineral interest in the Grant- Kohrs Ranch region stemmed from the discovery of gold in the southwestern corner of Powell County in 1852. Early placer strikes gave way to lode extraction in the early 1870s. The main period of mine production was between 1880 and 1907. By 1896, copper- bearing ores in the Anaconda- Butte mining district were the dominant resource in the upper Clark Fork River Valley (Johns 1994). Still, gold, silver, copper, lead, manganese, and zinc extraction operations were all active in the area during World War II with some renewed interest during the Korean War. Most of these operations closed as interest waned, prices dropped, and new environmental regulations were enacted in the 1980s. By 1983, the Anaconda smelter shut down, eliminating the sell- to point for mined ore (Power 1996). As a result, many mines were abandoned and/or declared inactive. These sites continue to pose negative impacts to the environment (Madison et al. 1998).

The U.S. Geological Survey defined sixteen mining districts in the upper Clark Fork River basin. These included: the Big Foot, Oro Fino, Pipestone, Homestake, Little Pipestone, Dunkleberg, Emery, Highland- Moose Creek, Pioneer (Gold Creek)- Rose Mountain, Racetrack, Red Lion, Silver Lake, Johnson Basin, Olson Gulch, Blue- Eyed Nellie, and Lost Creek districts (Madison et al. 1998). The estimated value of extracted minerals for these districts for combined gold, silver, copper, lead, and zinc totaled $15,106,170 at the time of production.

By the time extensive mining operations were in full force in the upper Clark Fork River valley, riparian vegetation was disappearing from stream and river banks. The loss of this buffering vegetation made the impact of seasonal flooding more severe and widespread. Erodable materials such as mine tailings were placed near streams and easily carried away by rising waters and redeposited in the floodplains. The largest recorded flood in the system occurred in 1908. This single event resulted in a 0.3 m (1 ft) thick deposit along the river in the Deer Lodge Valley. Toxic deposits from this and even earlier floods are called "slickens" and are visible today throughout the Deer Lodge Valley. These unvegetated, exposed piles are extremely vulnerable to erosion today.

Montana Lineament

West of Grant- Kohrs Ranch, the Clark Fork River valley forms part of the Montana Lineament or Lewis and Clark Line (Nimick 1993; Loan 2001). This feature is defined by a complex assortment of roughly parallel faults, folds, and linear valleys. It extends from northern Idaho (Coeur d'Alene mining district) to an area east of Helena, Montana and has a locally anomalous northwest to west- northwest trend (Loan 2001).

Despite some speculation on a Precambrian origin for the feature, most of the structures are late Cretaceous or younger and relate to the faulting associated with the late Laramide orogenic deformation (Loan 2001). Crustal movement along the Lewis and Clark line during the middle Eocene tilted the entire Garnet mountain range and changed the prevalent drainage system, leaving ancient stream gravels stranded hundreds of meters above the present Clark Fork River drainage (Reynolds and Sears 1989; Dundas 1990).

Map Unit Properties

This section provides a description for and identifies many characteristics of the map units that appear on the digital geologic map of Grant- Kohrs Ranch National Historic Site. The table is highly generalized and is provided for informational purposes only. Ground disturbing activities should not be permitted or denied on the basis of information contained in this table. More detailed unit descriptions can be found in the help files that accompany the digital geologic map or by contacting the NPS Geologic Resources Division.

Precambrian age rocks underlie the Grant- Kohrs Ranch area almost entirely. These rocks are part of the Belt Supergroup that is Late Proterozoic in age. These were deposited in an ancient marine basin. In the Deer Lodge Valley, these units are exposed on the western side, juxtaposed against Mesozoic and Cenozoic age rocks by a large range- bounding fault. Individual formations recognized among these older rocks include the Snowslip, Shepard, Mt. Shields, Bonner, McNamara, and Garnet Range units (Loan 2001).

The Jurassic Swift Formation and Cretaceous Golden Spike Formation are exposed north of the park. The Carter Creek and Kootenai formations are also present locally. These sedimentary units contain sandstone, mudstone, black shale, chert pebble conglomerate, rare limestone beds, and andesitic lava flows (Berg 2004).

The locally present Cretaceous Blackleaf Formation is a mixed unit of shales, sands, volcanoclastics, and silts deposited during marine transgression (Dyman et al. 1993). Many Cretaceous units were deposited during the regressions and transgressions of the Western Interior Seaway.

On the eastern side of Deer Lodge Valley are the Elkhorn Mountain Volcanics and other Cretaceous to Tertiary age basaltic flow units. These volcanic rock units are exposed over large areas of the map coverage.

The late Cretaceous to early Tertiary compressional Sevier–Laramide orogenic events caused huge blocks of buried rock to slide over younger rock in an easterly direction. These episodes caused the dramatic juxtaposition of rock ages found today at Grant- Kohrs Ranch.

Tertiary age sediments cover the central portion of the valley and result from local basins filling with sediments when extension along normal faults followed mountain building. These sediments consist of lacustrine beds, fluvial deposits, and ash beds. Extensive volcanism also accompanied extension and produced rhyolite tuffs interbedded with limestones, some intrusive dikes, and extensive ash beds. These sediments are as thick as 3,064 m (10,052 ft) 11 km (7 miles) south of Grant- Kohrs Ranch National Historic Site (Berg 2004).

Pleistocene glaciation and other geomorphological agents such as streams and landslides have all left recent, Quaternary age deposits on the landscape of the Deer Lodge Valley. Extensive terraces flank both sides of the Clark Fork River. Poorly sorted glacial till and outwash as well as slope deposits (landslides) and alluvial fans are present along the sides of the valley.

Large quantities of flood- deposited tailings are present throughout the Deer Lodge Valley. These deposits were derived from exposed and easily eroded mine and smelter waste and tailings. They are enriched in arsenic, cadmium, copper, iron, manganese, lead, and zinc (Smith et al. 1998). All of these contaminated deposits lie within the extensive 100- year floodplain of the upper Clark Fork River.

The following table presents a view of the stratigraphic column and an itemized list of features for each map unit. The table includes properties specific to each unit present in the stratigraphic column including map symbol, name, description, resistance to erosion, suitability for development, hazards, potential paleontologic resources, cultural and mineral resources, potential karst issues, recreational use potential, habitat, global significance, and limits on restoration.

Map Unit Properties Table

Age	Map Unit (Symbol)	Features and Description	Erosion Resistance	Suitability for Development	Hazards	Paleontological Resources	Potential Cultural Resources	Potential for Karst	Mineral Occurrence	Habitat	Recreation Potential	Global Significance	Limits on restoration
QUATERNARY (Holocene)	Sand and gravel pit (sg); Alluvial terrace deposit, youngest (Qal); Alluvial terrace deposit, 2nd youngest (Qatu); Alluvial terrace deposit, 3rd youngest (Qat2); Alluvial terrace deposit, 3rd youngest (Qat3)	Gravel, sand, silt, and clay along active river and creek channels; terrace deposits irregularly shaped, 1-5 m (3-6 ft) above current floodplain with poorly sorted clasts derived from Tertiary and older strata; older terraces contain similar clast deposits, but are higher above the floodplain, as much as 7-10 m (20-30 ft).	Low	Unconsolidated material underlies most valley areas of the park where buildings already exist and may heave with frost; high potential for groundwater and soil contamination in floodplain areas, should be avoided	Heavy metals in floodplain deposits derived from mine tailings could lead to contamination of groundwater, surface water, and soils; Unconsolidated deposits and tailing and other mill waste piles are associated with the potential for collapse and failure	None documented	Present land surface may contain Native American artifacts; history of landscape evolution related to ranching activities	None	Sand, gravel; acid mine drainage precipitates (heavy metals and oxides)	Riparian habitat along waterways	Good for trails, campgrounds	Terrace deposits date and define movement of the Clark Fork R.; floodplain deposits of heavy metals render the river area a Superfund site	Ground alteration activities could expose contaminated floodplain deposits
QUATERNARY (Pleistocene-Holocene)	Alluvium and colluvium (Qac); Landslide deposit (Qls); Alluvial fan deposit (Qaf); Alluvial terrace deposit, 4th youngest (Qat4); Alluvial terrace deposit, 5th youngest (Qat5)	Mixed slope and fluvial deposits; landslide deposits occur on some steeper slopes of Tertiary sedimentary rock; hummocky topography; contains poorly consolidated fine-grained rock and soil; alluvial fans consist of small deposits of gravel, sand, silt and clay along tributaries' boundary with the Clark Fork River floodplain; well developed on eastern shore. Poorly preserved terraces are moderately sorted and stratified above modern drainages, finer-grained than glacial deposits.	Low	Unconsolidated material flanking slopes along the valley edge may be too permeable for waste facilities and unstable for some building projects near slopes	Unconsolidated deposits are associated with high erodability, and the potential for collapse and failure	Some Pleistocene fossil assemblages present locally including shells, rodent bones, some larger mammal remains (Bison, Camelops, Equus, and Proboscidea)	Higher present land terraces may contain Native American campsites and artifacts	None	Sand, gravel	Upland terrace habitat for grazing animals	Good for trails, campgrounds	Terrace deposits date and define movement of the Clark Fork River	Unstable slopes may erode easily
QUATERNARY (Pleistocene – Holocene)	Glacial outwash deposit (Qgo); Glacial till (Qgt); Glacial till, older (Qgto); Pediment gravel deposit (Qpg); Glacial outwash of Bull Lake Glaciation (Qgob); Glacial till of Bull Lake Glaciation (Qgtb)	Poorly sorted, well rounded material ranging in size from sand and clay to boulders; outwash deposits primarily composed of volcanics on eastern side of valley; 80- 95% granitic clasts on western side. Percentage of quartzite clasts increases towards the Clark Fork River; till deposits mostly poorly sorted granitic material with little to no weathering noted; Scattered granite boulders are remnants of older till; pediment deposits are poorly stratified and range 0- 7 m (1- 20 ft) thk. with cobbles and pebbles ranging from east to west of volcanic rocks to metasedimentary rocks predominating, older glacial deposits and tills are poorly exposed, non- stratified or lithified, with a clay to sand matrix, and more weathered.	Low	Heterogeneous substrate may be unstable for building sites; dependent on abundance of clay; may be locally too permeable for waste facilities.	Unconsolidated deposits are associated with high erodability, and the potential for collapse and failure, with higher clay contents in till, slumping and slope creep are possible.		Most recent glacial deposits may contain artifacts and campsites from Native Americans	None	Sand, gravel, silt, and clay in unsorted deposits	Upland and fan deposits for grazing animal habitat	Good for trails and campgrounds unless very clay rich	Dates ice age events in the Deer Lodge Valley	Undercut areas are prone to slumping and sliding
TERTIARY	Sedimentary rocks, undivided (Ts); Ash bed (Tsa)	Massive deposits of sandy to silty mudstone with grayish- orange color; some sand, pebble conglomerate beds present locally with granite and quartzite clasts; some bentonite beds present locally; white ash beds form small resistant ledges 1 to 2 m (3- 6 ft) thick with sand size fragments.	Moderate	Altered volcanic clays and poorly cemented rock layers render this unit rather unstable for development, especially for roads and foundations	Resistant ledges may pose rockfall hazard; shrink and swell clays lead to instability	None documented	None documented	None	Volcanic ash	Resistant beds may provide ledges for mountain lions and birds	Good for most uses unless significant quantities of bentonite are present	Ash beds may date volcanic activity	Only if highly weathered

Age	Map Unit (Symbol)	Features and Description	Erosion Resistance	Suitability for Development	Hazards	Paleontological Resources	Potential Cultural Resources	Potential for Karst	Mineral Occurrence	Habitat	Recreation Potential	Global Significance	Limits on restoration
TERTIARY	Mafic to intermediate intrusive bodies (Tinii)	Dark-gray alkali basalt & andesite dikes intruding the Carter Creek Formation in the northwestern portion of the map coverage.	Moderate to high	Present only in local areas in limited extent	More erodable if undercut, rockfall potential	None	None documented	None	Metallic minerals may be associated with alkali volcanic rocks	Resistant beds may provide ledges for mountain lions and birds	Trails associated with this unit may be vulnerable to rockfall	Dates mafic igneous activity during the Tertiary	None known
TERTIARY	Rhyolite tuff, tuffaceous sediments, and fossiliferous limestone (Trt)	Tuffaceous rocks of white to buff-gray color containing sparse coarser grained tuff-breccia lenses and darker volcanic fragments; some interbedded fossiliferous limestone containing siliceous tuff in northwestern portion of map.	Moderate	Highly dissolvable limestone interbeds, if present, may render unit unstable for development, and too permeable for waste facilities	High potential for slides and rockfall if slope is present	Fossils present in limestone	None documented	Some limestone dissolution possible	Tuff breccia	Weathered limestone provides vugs for bird nests, ledges may provide cliff habitat	Interbeds can make unit weak as trail base, fine for most uses	Records volcanic activity in marine environment of Tertiary	None, unless limestone beds are highly weathered
CRETACEOUS	Golden Spike Formation (Kgs), Lava flow unit (informal) of the Golden Spike Formation (Kgsl)	Andesitic lava flows with some interbedded sandstone, conglomerate, and volcaniclastic deposits; minor limestone and black shale; fragments include quartz, biotite, muscovite, plagioclase, volcanic glass and assorted lithic fragments. In lava flows, plagioclase phenocrysts 3 mm to 1 cm locally abundant; some pyroxene phenocrysts; tops of some flows marked by flow breccias; flow banding locally defined by phenocrysts.	Moderate to high	Strong bedding with contrasting rock types in sharp contact may present structural weakness; competent enough for most uses.	Differing resistance to erosion increases possibility of rockfalls and slides	Possible fossils in limestone interbeds	None documented	Minor limestone dissolution possible	Hematite deposits at andesite–limestone contacts	Resistant beds may provide ledges for mountain lions and birds	Interbeds can make unit weak as trail base, fine for most uses	May date Cretaceous volcanic activity, includes flow indicators	None known
CRETACEOUS	Basalt flows and flow breccia (Kba), Basalt flows and flow breccias, large-pyroxene basalt (Kbpx); basalt flows and flow breccias, plagioclase basalt (Kbpl)	Massive basalt beds, poorly exposed, some contain augite phenocrysts as large as 1 cm in a dark-green matrix, plagioclase phenocrysts common in some layers.	Moderate	Present only in local areas in limited extent	Rough surface locally, could pose walking hazard	None	Phenocrysts may have been used as decorative elements	None	Augite and plagioclase phenocrysts	None documented	Fine for most uses, rough trail base	May date Cretaceous volcanic activity	None known
CRETACEOUS	Elkhorn Mountains Volcanics (Kem); Welded ash-flow tuff (Kent); Andesitic lava flows (Kemf); Tuff and tuff breccia (Kemtb); Andesite flows, flow breccia and tuff breccia (Kemfb)	Brownish-red tuff with abundant lithic fragments (mostly andesite), but sparse crystals; some dark green, fine-grained flows present; tuffs contain white andesitic flows in dark gray-green groundmass; andesitic flows and tuffs are dark gray to purple with white, flattened plagioclase phenocrysts ("oatmeal andesite").	Moderate	Good for most uses unless pervasive vesicles and fractures are present	Rough surface locally, could pose walking hazard, differential erosion may lead to rockfall potential	None	Phenocrysts may have been used as decorative elements	None	"Oatmeal andesite" formed by large plagioclase phenocrysts	None documented	Fine for most uses	May date Cretaceous igneous activity	None known

Age	Map Unit (Symbol)	Features and Description	Erosion Resistance	Suitability for Development	Hazards	Paleontological Resources	Potential Cultural Resources	Potential for Karst	Mineral Occurrence	Habitat	Recreation Potential	Global Significance	Limits on restoration
CRETACEOUS	Carter Creek Formation (Kcc)	North part of map; consists of coarse-grained, cross-bedded sandstone with some light-colored tuffaceous interbeds and brownish-gray limestone lenses; locally more than 150 m (500 ft) thick.	Moderate to high	Good for most uses unless thin bedding is present, providing planes of weakness in the rock column; mostly exposed at higher elevations.	Sandstone may be undercut leading to rockfall situations at the bases of slopes	None described in limestones	None documented	Minor limestone beds possibly dissolved	Sandstone	Resistant beds may provide ledges for mountain lions and birds	Interbeds and fracturing can make unit vulnerable to rockfall, fine for most uses	None documented	None known
CRETACEOUS	Kootenai Formation (Kk)	Consists locally of four units; from bottom to top: calcareous, upper clastic, gastropod limestone, and upper quartzite members.	Moderate to high	Good for most uses unless pervasive dissolution is present and/or quartzite beds are undercut rendering them unstable	Potential for rockfall where quartzite is undercut by dissolved limestone	Gastropods found in middle to upper beds	None documented	Potential exists for small caves	Quartzite	Weathered limestone may create vugs for nests	Rockfall potential for trails if unit is undercut, fine for most uses	Cretaceous fossils from Western Interior Seaway	None, unless highly weathered
JURASSIC	Swift Formation (Jsw)	Predominantly sandstone beds of light gray, tan and pink color; contains quartz veins that locally comprise more than 50% of the rock mass; chert clasts (up to 3 cm in diameter) and chert pebble conglomerate lenses also locally present.	High	Good for most uses unless highly fractured or jointed, providing planes of weakness in the rock column; mostly exposed at higher elevations	If highly jointed or fractured and exposed on a slope, rockfall and slides possible	None documented	Large chert clasts may have provided tool material	None	Chert nodules, conglomerate and sandstone	Resistant beds may provide cliffs and ledges for mountain lions and birds	Interbeds and fracturing can make unit vulnerable to rockfall, fine for most uses	None documented	None known
MESOZOIC - PALEOZOIC	Mesozoic and Paleozoic sedimentary beds (MPzs)	Not exposed in Grant-Kohrs NHS; used only in cross section.	NA	NA	NA	NA	NA	NA	NA	NA	NA	Record of Paleozoic and Mesozoic tectono-climatic history in region	NA
PROTEROZOIC	Belt Supergroup undivided (Ybe)	Metasedimentary rocks including siltite, argillaceous quartzite, and quartzites present in northern areas of map coverage.	Moderate to high	Good for most uses unless thin bedding is present, providing planes of weakness in the rock column. Mostly exposed at higher elevations.	If highly jointed or fractured and exposed on a slope, rockfall and slides possible	Possible stromatolites in carbonate units	None, unless igneous, ore-bearing veins are present	Potential in carbonate units	Salt casts, veins, some calcite	Provides high elevation habitat for birds of prey and other animals	Fine for all uses	Extensive, preserved Precambrian sedimentary rocks	Exposed locally

Geologic History

This section highlights the map units (i.e., rocks and unconsolidated deposits) that occur in Grant-Kohrs Ranch National Historic Site and puts them in a geologic context in terms of the environment in which they were deposited and the timing of geologic events that created the present landscape.

The known geologic history of Grant-Kohrs Ranch begins in the Proterozoic Eon (see figure 3). Little is known about this period of earth's history. Most rocks on earth of Precambrian age are deformed and metamorphosed, losing most, if not all traces of their original structures. Western Montana, however, hosts one of the most well preserved Precambrian sedimentary records on earth.

The Proterozoic rocks in the Deer Lodge Valley are part of the Belt Supergroup. This name refers to a stack of rocks formed in the ancient Belt basin that covered large parts of Montana, Idaho, Alberta, and Washington. The Belt basin formed in response to high angle faulting and subsidence of large continental basement blocks of rock, veneered by a discontinuous blanket of quartz sand. Dark quartzite, argillite, and carbonate of lower Belt formations mark the first and most extensive spread of the great Belt lake over basement crystalline rocks (Winston 1989b).

Perhaps the most striking tectonic event during lower Belt deposition was block faulting along the Perry line, which uplifted the Dillon crustal block of the Archean Wyoming province to the south and downdropped crustal rocks to the north, forming the southern margin of the basin (figures 4 and 5). The resulting eastern indentation is called the Helena embayment and comprises an arm of the Belt basin. The basin extended across western Montana, northern Idaho, and into eastern Washington (Winston 1989b).

From the relatively undisturbed, subaqueous, evenly layered deposits of the lower Belt formations, the upward transition into ripple-marked, mud-cracked redbeds indicates progradation of playas and alluvial aprons from the west across the Belt basin (Winston 1989b). In other words, this transition shows the advance of continental environments, as opposed to marine, broadly across the basin. Sea level continued to fluctuate throughout the late Proterozoic.

Many formations within the Belt Supergroup are widespread, extending from eastern Washington to east of Grant-Kohrs Ranch National Historic Site. This shows that, during its maximum spread, the Belt sea had a fetch of more than 300 km (186 mi), without including the western edge of the basin. This basin is inferred to be comparable in scale to the northern part of the modern Caspian Sea (Winston and Lyons 1993).

The uppermost beds of the group record cyclic changes in sea level. During lowstand conditions, the variety of shoreline environments included: 1) braided flood channels filled with cross-bedded sand; 2) shallow sheet-flood tracks; 3) shallow ponds with mud layers and small-scale ripple marks; 4) exposed, desiccated mudflats, vulnerable to rip-ups during occasional floods; 5) broad sand flats; and 6) beaches. These shoreline environments moved progressively basinward in periods of transgression and retreated from the basin towards the craton during periods of regression.

Throughout the Paleozoic Era, Africa, and South America were approaching North America as the two great landmasses, Laurasia and Gondwana, collided. The ancient continent of Gondwana included Australia, Antarctica, Africa, South America, and India south of the Ganges River, plus smaller islands. Laurasia, located in the northern hemisphere contained the present northern continents. The union of Gondwana and Laurasia formed the supercontinent, Pangaea, which was centered on the equator.

In the early Cambrian Period, the region again underwent uplift and erosion. Following the uplift, the region subsided and an ancient sea advanced bringing with it the depositional environments necessary to capture vast amounts of sediments. By Late Cambrian time, marine waters covered virtually all of Montana and Idaho. The equator ran through the length of Idaho, and carbonate muds accumulated under these warm-water conditions in much the same way as they do in the broad carbonate-mud shoal-bank area of the Bahaman Islands today (Hintze 1988).

In the Early-Middle Devonian Period (about 401 Ma), the first compressive pulses of the Antler Orogeny in the west and the Acadian Orogeny in the east (part of the Appalachian Orogeny) began as landmasses accreted onto both the western and eastern borders of North America.

To the west of Montana, a subduction zone formed and lithospheric plates collided against one another bending, buckling, folding, and faulting into a north-south trending mountain range that stretched from Nevada to Canada.

During orogenic events, great sheets of rocks measuring tens to hundreds of kilometers in width and length are stacked on top of one another. The weight of this rock depresses the land in front of the stack, or foreland area, and causes the foreland to subside into a foreland basin. As the highlands to the west were thrust above sea level at the beginning of the Mississippian, warm marine water flooded the foreland basin and spread over southeastern Idaho and western Montana giving rise to an extensive carbonate platform.

The sea became shallower during the regression that followed the Antler Orogeny. The area transitioned into a broad karst plain of shallow- marine sandstone and micrite (carbonate mudstone), and by the end of the Mississippian, the area was again exposed to subaerial erosion (Poole and Sandberg 1991; Graham et al. 2002). Coincident with Pennsylvanian tectonics was a global climate shift from the warm humid environment of the Late Mississippian to a more arid environment in the region of Idaho during the Early Pennsylvanian (Rueger 1996).

As the Ancestral Rocky Mountains formed, the Ouachita- Marathon thrustbelt, the Anadarko Basin, and other Permian basins developed. From the Pennsylvanian to Middle Permian time, shallow stagnant seas persisted over most of the region (Baker and Crittenden 1961). Across the globe, the Permian Period appears to have been a time of dramatic environmental change.

The Permian equator was oriented southwest- northeast through present- day Wyoming and eastern Utah. An arid climate prevailed in this western part of the supercontinent Pangaea and resulted in restricted marine evaporitic conditions over much of the cratonic shelf seaway (Peterson 1980; Graham *et al.* 2002).

From rock deposits around the globe, geologists have documented the third, and most severe, major mass extinction of geologic time at the close of the Permian. Although not as well known as the extinction event that exterminated the dinosaurs at the end of the Mesozoic, the Permian extinction was much more extensive.

Throughout the Triassic and Jurassic, periodic incursions from the north brought shallow seas flooding into Wyoming, Montana, and a northeast- southwest trending trough on the Utah and Idaho border. Volcanoes formed an arcuate north- south chain of mountains off the western coast in what is now central Nevada. To the south, the landmass that would become South America was splitting away from the Texas coast just as Africa and Great Britain were rifting away from the present East Coast and opening up the Atlantic Ocean.

The Western Interior Basin was a broad, shallow, asymmetric basin on the southwest side of the North American craton during this time. The basin stretched

northward from its southern margin in Arizona and New Mexico across the Canadian border.

The next major tectonic event to leave its mark on the Grant- Kohrs Ranch area was regional compression. This resulted in the uplift of thousands of meters of sedimentary deposits buried in the basin covering western Montana. This event is known as the Sevier-Laramide orogeny. First, the Sevier orogeny was characterized by relatively thin slabs of older, upper Precambrian and lower Paleozoic sedimentary rocks being shoved eastward, over younger, upper Paleozoic and lower Mesozoic rocks. Later, the Laramide orogeny involved thick, basement- cored uplifts along shallowing downward thrust faults, and extensive folding.

As the mountains rose in the west and the roughly north- south trending trough east of those highlands expanded, the Gulf of Mexico, separating North and South America, continued to rift open in the south. Marine water spilled northward into the basin. At the same time, marine water transgressed from the Arctic region.

The seas advanced and retreated many times during the Cretaceous until the most extensive interior seaway ever recorded drowned much of western North America. The Western Interior Seaway was an elongate basin that extended from today's Gulf of Mexico to the Arctic Ocean, a distance of about 4,827 km (3,000 mi) (Kauffman 1977). During periods of maximum transgression, the width of the basin was 1,600 km (1,000 mi) from western Utah to western Iowa. The basin was relatively unrestricted at either end (Kauffman 1977).

For about 35 million years during the Laramide Orogeny, from roughly 70 Ma to 35 Ma, the collision of tectonic plates transformed the extensive basin of the Cretaceous Interior Seaway into smaller interior basins bordered by rugged mountains (anticlines and synclines on the scale of miles) (Ehrlich 1999; Graham et al. 2002). These mountains were the focus of intense erosion and weathering, resulting in basin infilling across the region during the Tertiary.

Following extensive crustal thickening during the Laramide orogeny, melting of the lower crust occurred during decompression. This gave rise to the material of the Tertiary Boulder Batholith and the intrusions associated with mineral deposits found near Grant-Kohrs Ranch. The emplacement of these intrusions was facilitated by mantle upwelling and underplating of a hot lower crust during the regional crustal extension that followed decompression (Cunningham 1971; Vogel et al. 1997). Near the end of the Laramide Orogeny, in early mid- Tertiary time, volcanic activity erupted across the area, depositing the volcanic rocks in the present Deer Lodge Valley (Baars 2000; Fillmore 2000).

The deformational regime changed once again from compressional to extensional. The southwestern margin of North America underwent extensional deformation.

As the crust was extended, movement along normal faults such as the Mount Powell fault accommodated crustal tension (Konizeski et al. 1968). When one block of rock falls relative to another, the resulting graben valley forms a substantial sediment sink.

Accompanying the extension of the crust during the Tertiary, normal fault- bounded valleys filled with a variety of sediments shed from the newly exposed highlands. In the Grant- Kohrs area, during and after a period of intense regional erosion that probably occupied much of the Eocene and early Oligocene, pediments (erosion surfaces) formed throughout the valley (Konizeski et al. 1968). These surfaces are characterized by a variety of sediments ranging from sandstone, mudstone, limestone, and coal to volcanic ash deposits. This assortment reflects the tectonic and climatic variations during the Tertiary.

The Quaternary Period is subdivided into two epochs: 1) the Pleistocene, which ranges from about 1.6 Ma to 10,000 years before present (B.P.), and 2) the younger Holocene Epoch that extends from 10,000 years B.P. to the present. The Pleistocene Epoch is known as the Ice Age and is marked by multiple episodes of continental and alpine glaciation.

During the Pleistocene great continental glaciers, thousands of feet thick, advanced and retreated in approximately 100,000- year cycles. Huge volumes of water were stored in the glaciers during glacial periods causing sea level to drop as much as 91 m (300 ft) (Fillmore 2000). Glacial deposits of till, outwash, and moraines are all present in the Deer Lodge Valley attesting to glacial conditions in the area (figure 6).

The glacial deposits from the Pleistocene and Holocene and recent alluvial terrace, valley fill, and gravel deposits along the streams and rivers, represent Quaternary age processes at Grant- Kohrs Ranch National Historic Site (Konizeski et al. 1968). Landslide and slope deposits are also prevalent in recent sediments due to the relief along terraces.

Eon	Era	Period	Epoch	Ma	Life Forms	N. American Tectonics
Phanerozoic (Phaneros = "evident"; zoic = "life")	Cenozoic	Quaternary	Recent, or Holocene		Age of Mammals — Modern man	Cascade volcanoes
				0.8	Extinction of large mammals and birds	Worldwide glaciation
			Pleistocene	1.8		
		Tertiary	Pliocene		Large carnivores	Uplift of Sierra Nevada
				5.3	Whales and apes	Linking of N. & S. America
			Miocene	23.8		
			Oligocene	33.7		Basin-and-Range Extension
			Eocene	55.5		Laramide orogeny ends (West)
			Paleocene		Early primates	
				65		
	Mesozoic	Cretaceous			Age of Dinosaurs — Mass extinctions	Laramide orogeny (West)
					Placental mammals	Sevier orogeny (West)
				145	Early flowering plants	Nevadan orogeny (West)
		Jurassic			First mammals	Elko orogeny (West)
				213	Flying reptiles	Breakup of Pangea begins
		Triassic			First dinosaurs	Sonoma orogeny (West)
				248		
	Paleozoic	Permian			Age of Amphibians — Mass extinctions	Super continent Pangea intact
					Coal-forming forests diminish	Ouachita orogeny (South)
						Alleghenian (Appalachian) orogeny (East)
				286		Ancestral Rocky Mts. (West)
		Pennsylvanian			Coal-forming swamps	
				325	Sharks abundant	
		Mississippian			Variety of insects	
				360	First amphibians	
		Devonian			First reptiles	Antler orogeny (West)
					Fishes — Mass extinctions	
				410	First forests (evergreens)	Acadian orogeny (East-NE)
		Silurian		440	First land plants	
		Ordovician			Marine Invertebrates — Mass extinctions	
					First primitive fish	
					Trilobite maximum	Taconic orogeny (NE)
				505	Rise of corals	
		Cambrian				Avalonian orogeny (NE)
					Early shelled organisms	Extensive oceans cover most of N. America
				544		
Proterozoic ("Early life")		Precambrian			1st multicelled organisms	Formation of early supercontinent
						First iron deposits
					Jellyfish fossil (670Ma)	Abundant carbonate rocks
Archean ("Ancient")				2500		
					Early bacteria & algae	
				~3800		Oldest known Earth rocks (~3.93 billion years ago)
Hadean ("Beneath the Earth")					Origin of life?	Oldest moon rocks (4-4.6 billion years ago)
						Earth's crust being formed
				4600	Formation of the Earth	

Figure 3. Geologic time scale; adapted from the U.S. Geological Survey. Red lines indicate major unconformities between eras. Included are major events in life history and tectonic events occurring on the North American continent. Absolute ages shown are in millions of years.

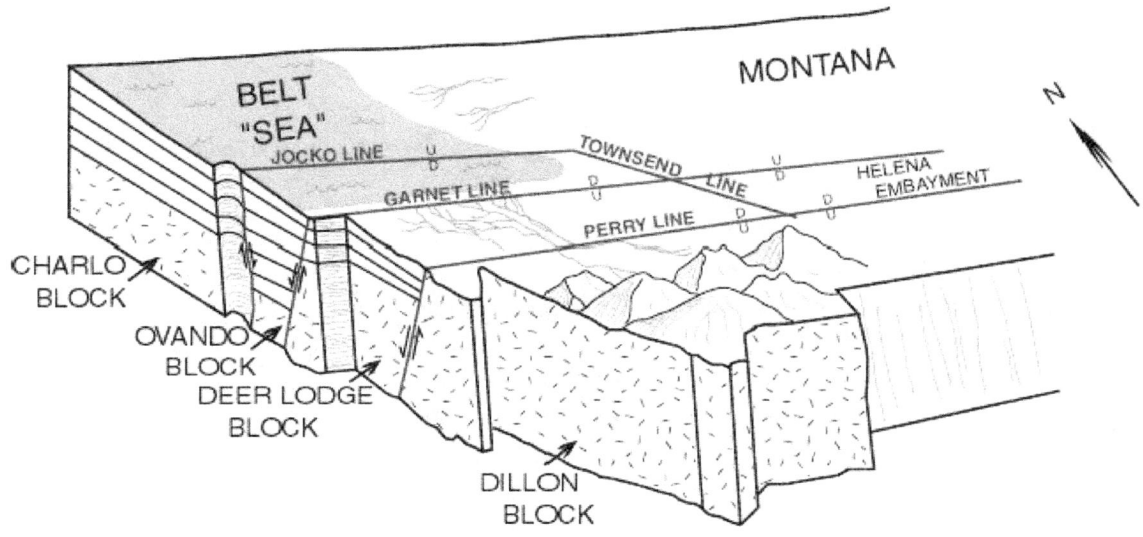

Figure 4. Showing inferred Proterozoic structure of the Belt basin during Late Belt Supergroup deposition. Note numerous faults providing means for uplift south of the basin (sediment source area). "U" indicates the uplifted side of the fault, and "D" indicates the downdropped side. Modified from Ackman 1988.

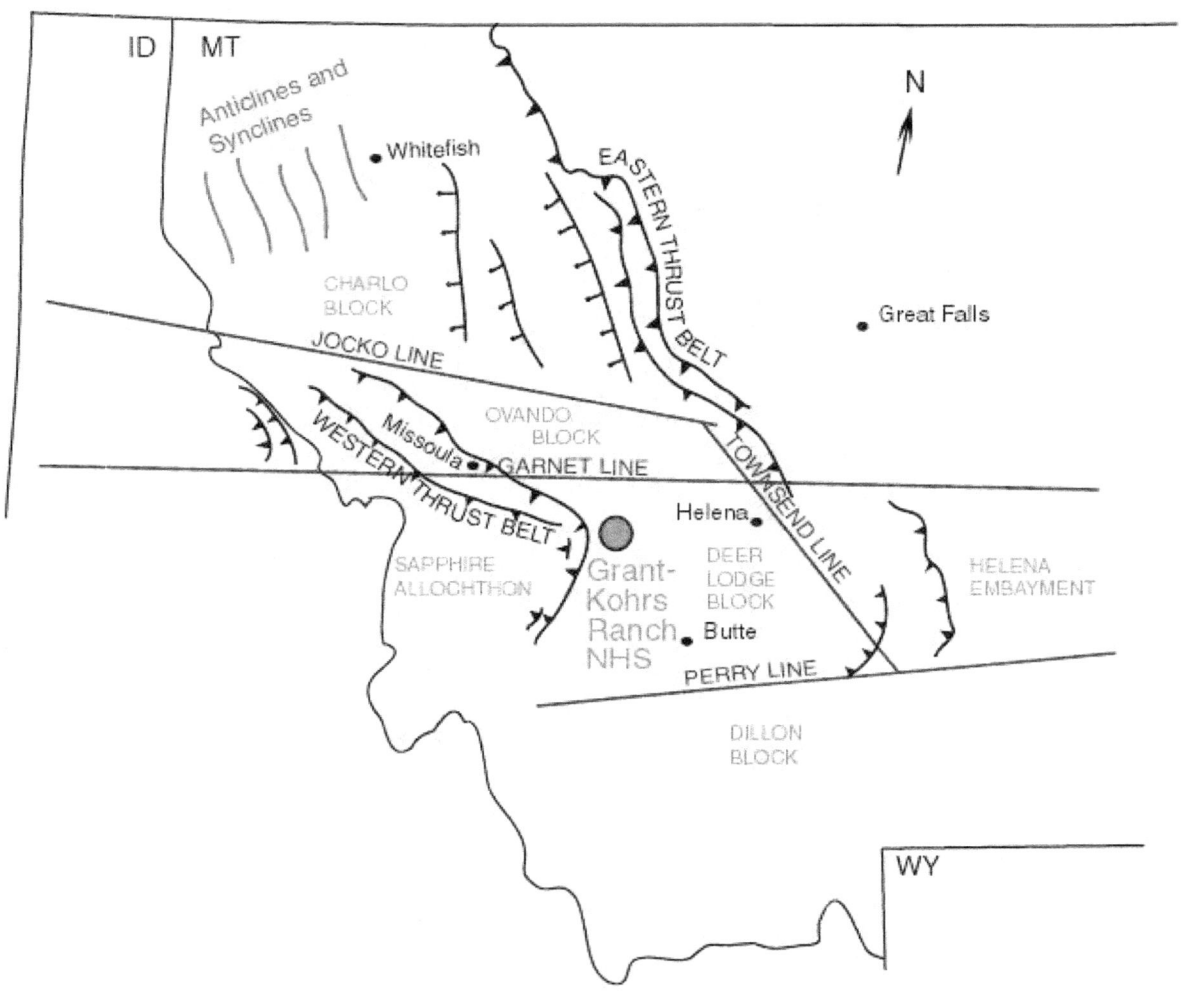

Figure 5. Map of present day structural features in the Grant-Kohrs Ranch area superimposed on Mid-Proterozoic fault lines (blue) with cratonic blocks labeled in green. Red lines indicate fold axes, black lines with teeth indicate thrust faults with teeth on overriding plate, black lines with bar and ball show normal faults with the symbol on the downthrown block. Adapted from Winston 1989.

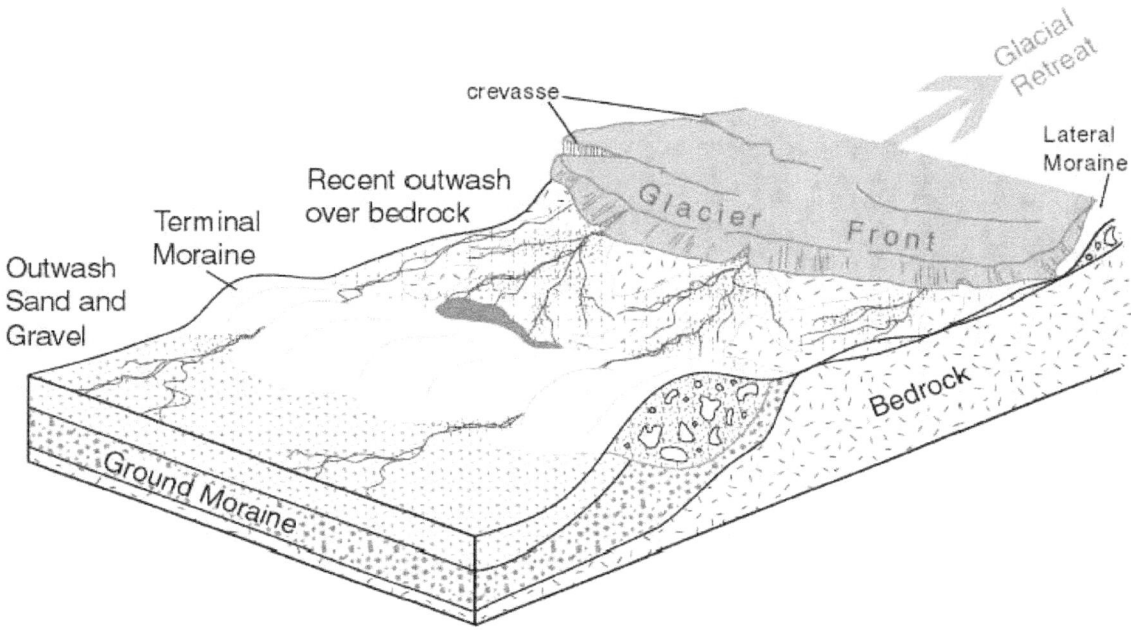

Figure 6. Diagrammatic view of a retreating glacier with a recent terminal moraine and a broad space between the moraine and the glacier front. Note the variety of deposits associated with glacial melt many of which exist on the landscape at Grant-Kohrs Ranch National Historic Site.

Glossary

This glossary contains brief definitions of technical geologic terms used in this report. Not all geologic terms used are referenced. For more detailed definitions or to find terms not listed here please visit: http://wrgis.wr.usgs.gov/docs/parks/misc/glossarya.html.

alluvium. Stream- deposited sediment that is generally rounded, sorted, and stratified.

aquifer. Rock or sediment that are sufficiently porous, permeable, and saturated to be useful as a source of water.

ash (volcanic). Fine pyroclastic material ejected from a volcano (also see tuff).

basement. The undifferentiated rocks, commonly igneous and metamorphic, that underlie the rocks of interest.

basin (structural). A doubly- plunging syncline in which rocks dip inward from all sides.

basin (sedimentary). Any depression, from continental to local scales, into which sediments are deposited.

batholith. A massive, discordant pluton, greater than 100 km², (39.6 mi²) often formed from multiple intrusions.

bed. The smallest sedimentary strata unit, commonly ranging in thickness from one centimeter to a meter or two and distinguishable from beds above.

block (fault). A crustal unit bounded by faults, either completely or in part.

cementation. Chemical precipitation of material into pores between grains that bind the grains into rock.

clastic. Rock or sediment made of fragments or pre- existing rocks.

clay. Clay minerals or sedimentary fragments the size of clay minerals (<2 cm).

conglomerate. A coarse- grained sedimentary rock with clasts larger than 2 mm in a fine- grained matrix.

craton. The relatively old and geologically stable interior of a continent (also see continental shield).

cross-bedding. Uniform to highly- varied sets of inclined sedimentary beds deposited by wind or water that indicate distinctive flow conditions.

cross section. A graphical interpretation of geology, structure, and/or stratigraphy in the third (vertical) dimension based on mapped and measured geological extents and attitudes depicted in an oriented vertical plane.

deformation. A general term for the process of faulting, folding, shearing, extension, or compression of rocks as a result of various Earth forces.

dike. A tabular, discordant igneous intrusion.

dip. The angle between a structural surface and a horizontal reference plane measured normal to their line of intersection.

drainage basin. The total area from which a stream system receives or drains precipitation runoff.

extrusive. Of or pertaining to the eruption of igneous material onto the surface of Earth.

fault. A subplanar break in rock along which relative movement occurs between the two sides.

formation. Fundamental rock- stratigraphic unit that is mappable and lithologically distinct from adjoining strata and has definable upper and lower contacts.

fracture. Irregular breakage of a mineral; also any break in a rock (e.g., crack, joint, fault)

graben. A down- dropped structural block bounded by steeply- dipping, normal faults (also see horst).

horst. An uplifted structural block bounded by high- angle normal faults.

igneous. Refers to a rock or mineral that originated from molten material; one of the three main classes or rocks: igneous, metamorphic, and sedimentary.

intrusion. A body of igneous rock that invades older rock. The invading rock may be a plastic solid or magma that pushes its way into the older rock.

joint. A semi- planar break in rock without relative movement of rocks on either side of the fracture surface.

lacustrine. Pertaining to, produced by, or inhabiting a lake or lakes.

landslide. Any process or landform resulting from rapid mass movement under relatively dry conditions.

levees. Raised ridges lining the banks of a stream; may be natural or artificial.

lineament. Any relatively straight surface feature that can be identified via observation, mapping, or remote sensing, often representing tectonic features.

lithology. The description of a rock or rock unit, especially the texture, composition, and structure of sedimentary rocks.

lithosphere. The relatively rigid outmost shell of Earth's structure, 50 to 100 km (31 to 62 mi) thick, that encompasses the crust and uppermost mantle.

mantle. The zone of Earth's interior between crust and core.

matrix. The fine- grained interstitial material between coarse grains in porphyritic igneous rocks and poorly sorted clastic sediments or rocks.

meanders. Sinuous lateral curves or bends in a stream's channel.

metamorphism. Literally, "change in form". Metamorphism occurs in rocks with mineral alteration, genesis, and/or recrystallization from increased heat and pressure.

mud cracks. Cracks formed in clay, silt, or mud by shrinkage during subaerial dehydration.

nonconformity. An erosional surface preserved in strata in which crystalline igneous or metamorphic rocks underlie sedimentary rocks.

normal fault. A dip- slip fault in which the hanging wall moves down relative to the footwall.

orogeny. A mountain- building event, particularly a well-recognized event in the geological past (e.g. the Laramide orogeny).

outcrop. Any part of a rock mass or formation that is exposed or "crops out" at Earth's surface.

outwash. Glacial sediment transported and deposited by meltwater streams.

overbank deposits. Alluvium deposited outside a stream channel during flooding.

Pangaea. A theoretical, single supercontinent that existed during the Permian and Triassic Periods

pebble. Generally, small, rounded, rock particles from 4 to 64 mm in diameter.

pediment. A gently sloping, erosional bedrock surface at the foot of mountains or plateau escarpments.

permeability. A measure of the ease or rate that fluids move through rocks or sediments.

plateau. A broad, flat- topped topographic high of great extent and elevation above the surrounding plains, canyons, or valleys (both land and marine landforms).

plate tectonics. The theory that the lithosphere is broken up into a series of rigid plates that move over Earth's surface above a more fluid aesthenosphere.

point bar. A sand and gravel ridge deposited in a stream channel on the inside of a meander where flow velocity slows.

porosity. The proportion of void space (cracks, interstices) in a volume of a rock or sediment.

regression. A long- term seaward retreat of the shoreline or rrelative fall of sea level.

reverse fault. A contractional, high angle (>45°), dip- slip fault in which the hanging wall moves up relative to the footwall (also see thrust fault).

ripple marks. The undulating, subparallel, usually small-scale, ridge pattern formed on sediment by the flow of wind or water.

sandstone. Clastic sedimentary rock of predominantly sand- sized grains.

scarp. A steep cliff or topographic step resulting from vertical displacement on a fault or by mass movement.

sediment. An eroded and deposited, unconsolidated accumulation of lithic and mineral fragments.

sedimentary rock. A consolidated and lithified rock consisting of detrital and/or chemical sediment(s).

shale. A clastic sedimentary rock made of clay- sized particles that exhibit parallel splitting properties.

silt. Clastic sedimentary material intermediate in size between fine- grained sand and coarse clay (1/256- 1/16 mm).

siltstone. A variable- lithified sedimentary rock with silt-sized grains.

slump. A generally large, coherent mass movement with a concave- up failure surface and subsequent backward rotation relative to the slope.

stratigraphy. The geologic study of the origin, occurrence, distribution, classification, correlation, age, etc. of rock layers, especially sedimentary rocks.

strike. The compass direction of the line of intersection that an inclined surface makes with a horizontal plane.

strike-slip fault. A fault with measurable offset where the relative movement is parallel to the strike of the fault.

subsidence. The gradual sinking or depression of part of Earth's surface.

tectonic. Relating to large- scale movement and deformation of Earth's crust.

terraces. Step- like benches surrounding the present floodplain of a stream due to dissection of previous flood plain(s), stream bed(s), and/or valley floor(s).

thrust fault. A contractional, dip- slip fault with a shallowly dipping fault surface (<45°) where the hanging wall moves up and over relative to the footwall.

transgression. Landward migration of the sea due to a relative rise in sea level.

trend. The direction or azimuth of elongation or a linear geological feature.

tuff. Generally fine- grained, igneous rock formed of consolidated volcanic ash.

unconformity. A surface within sedimentary strata that marks a prolonged period of nondeposition or erosion.

volcanic. Related to volcanoes; describes igneous rock crystallized at or near Earth's surface (e.g., lava).

water table. The upper surface of the saturated (phreatic) zone.

weathering. The set of physical, chemical, and biological processes by which rock is broken down in place.

References

This section provides a listing of references cited in this report. It also contains general references that may be of use to resource managers. A more complete geologic bibliography is available and can be obtained through the NPS Geologic Resources Division.

Baars, D. L. 2000. *The Colorado Plateau.* Albuquerque, NM: University of New Mexico press.

Baker, A.A., M.D. Crittenden, Jr. 1961. *Geology of the Timpanogos Cave Quadrangle, Utah.* U.S. Geological Survey, Geologic Quadrangle Map - Report: GQ- 0132.

Bedunah, D., T. Jones. 2001. *Flood Plain Vegetation Changes on the Grant- Kohrs Ranch National Historic Site Between 1993 and 2000.* http://www.nps.gov/archive/grko/Vegetation%20Changes.pdf (accessed January 20, 2007).

Berg, R.B. 2004. *Geologic Map of the Deer Lodge and Conleys Lake 7 ½' Quadrangles, Powell County, Southwestern Montana.* Montana Bureau of Mines and Geology Open File Report 509.

Breuninger, A.B. 2000. *Effects of floodplain remediation on bed sediment contamination in the Upper Clark Fork River basin, western Montana.* Master's thesis: University of Montana.

Butler, J.A. 2003. Metal contamination of the Clark Fork River, western Montana; a comparative study of metal concentrations in fine- grained bed sediment and source material. *Abstracts with Programs - Geological Society of America* 35 (5): 7.

Cunningham, F.F. 1971. The Silent City of Rocks, a bornhardt landscape in the Cotterrel Range, South Idaho, USA. *Zeitschrift fuer Geomorphologie* 15 (4): 404- 429.

Dodge, K.A., M.I. Hornberger, I.R. Lavigne. 2003. *Water- quality, bed- sediment, and biological data (October 2001 through September 2002) and statistical summaries of data for streams in the upper Clark Fork Basin, Montana.* U. S. Geological Survey, Open- File Report: OF 03- 0356.

Dodge, K.A., M.I. Hornberger, I.R. Lavigne. 2004. *Water- quality, bed- sediment and biological data (October 2002 through September 2003) and statistical summaries of data for streams in the upper Clark Fork Basin, Montana.* U. S. Geological Survey, Open- File Report: OF 2004- 1340.

Duaime, T.E., R.A. Appleman. 1990. *Storm- event monitoring on the upper Clark Fork River basin, Silver Bow and Deer Lodge counties.* MBMG Open- File Report: 228.

Dundas, R.G. 1990. Paleontology and geology of the late Pleistocene Hoover Creek terrace, Granite and Powell counties, Montana. *Northwest Geology* 19: 31- 37.

Dyman, T.S., R.G. Tysdal, C.A. Wallace, S.E. Lewis. 1993. Correlation chart of Lower and Lower- Upper Cretaceous Blackleaf Formation, eastern Pioneer Mountains, southwestern Montana, to Drummond, central- western Montana. *AAPG Bulletin* 77 (8): 1446.

Ehrlich, T.K. 1999. *Fault analysis and regional balancing of Cenozoic deformation in northwest Colorado and south- central Wyoming.* Master's thesis: Colorado State University.

Fillmore, R. 2000. *The Geology of the Parks, Monuments and Wildlands of Southern Utah.* The University of Utah Press.

Graham, J. P., T.L. Thornberry, S.A. O'Meara. 2002 (unpublished). *Geologic Resources Inventory for Mesa Verde National Park.* National Park Service, Fort Collins, CO: Inventory and Monitoring Program.

Hintze, L.F. 1988. *Geologic history of Utah.* Brigham Young University Geologic Studies, Special Publications: 7.

Hornberger, M.I., J.H. Lambing, S.N. Luoma, E.V. Axtmann. 1997. *Spatial and temporal trends of trace metals in surface water, bed sediment, and biota of the upper Clark Fork Basin, Montana, 1985- 95.* U. S. Geological Survey - Open- File Report: OF 97- 0669.

I.H. 2007. The Effects of Heavy Metal Toxicity. Incredible Horizons Digestive Problems Page, http://www.incrediblehorizons.com/toxicity%20&%20Autistic- symtoms.chelating.htm (accessed January 20, 2007).

Johns, C. 1995. Contamination of riparian wetlands from past copper mining and smelting in the headwaters region of the Clark Fork River, Montana, U.S.A. *Journal of Geochemical Exploration* 52, (1- 2): pp. 193- 203.

Kauffman, E. G. 1977. Geological and biological overview: Western Interior Cretaceous Basin: *Mountain Geologist* 14: 75- 99.

Konizeski, R.L., R.G. McMurtrey, A. Brietkrietz, A. 1968. *Geology and ground- water resources of the Deer Lodge Valley, Montana.* U. S. Geological Survey Water- Supply Paper: 1968.

Lonn, J. 2001. Floater's guide to the belt rocks of Alberton Gorge, western Montana. *Northwest Geology* 20: 51- 61.

Madison, J.P., J.D. Lonn, R.K. Marvin, J.J. Metesh, R. Wintergerst. 1998. *Abandoned- inactive mines program, Deer Lodge National Forest; Volume IV, Upper Clark Fork River drainage.* MBMG Open- File Report.

Moore, J.N., W.W. Woessner. 2000. *Geologic, Soil Water and Groundwater Report - 2000, Grant- Kohrs Ranch National Historic Site.* Department of the Interior, U.S. National Park Service.

Nimick, D.A. 1990. *Stratigraphy and chemistry of metal- contaminated floodplain sediments, upper Clark Fork River valley, Montana.* Master's thesis: University of Montana, Master's thesis.

Nimick, D.A. 1993. *Hydrology and water chemistry of shallow aquifers along the upper Clark Fork, western Montana.* U. S. Geological Survey, Water- Resources Investigations: WRI 93- 4052.

Nimick, D.A., J.N. Moore. 1994. Environmental chemistry of fluvially deposited mine tailings in the upper Clark Fork Valley, Montana. *Eos, Transactions, American Geophysical Union* 75 (44): 237.

Nimick, D.A., J.N. Moore. 1994. Stratigraphy and chemistry of sulfidic flood- plain sediments in the upper Clark Fork Valley, Montana. *ACS Symposium Series* 550: 276- 288.

Peterson, J. A. 1980. Permian paleogeography and sedimentary provinces, west central United States. In Thomas D. Fouch and Esther R. Magathan, eds., *Paleozoic Paleogeography of the West- Central United States,* eds. Fouch, T.D., E.R. Magathan, 271- 292. Rocky Mountain Section, SEPM (Society for Sedimentary Geology.

Poole, F. G., C.A. Sandberg. 1991. Mississippian paleogeography and conodont biostratigraphy of the western United States. In *Paleozoic Paleogeography of the Western United States – II,* eds. Cooper, J.D., C.H. Stevens, 107- 136. Society of Economic Paleontologists and Mineralogists (SEPM), Pacific Section.

Power, T.M. 1996. The Wealth of Nature. *Issues in Science and Technology.* http://www.findarticles.com/p/articles/mi_qa3622/is_1 99604/ai_n8743214/pg_1 (accessed January 21, 2007).

Rasmussen, D.L., R.W. Fields. 1980. Road log No. 1; Missoula to Flint Creek via upper Clark Fork valley and Drummond. *State of Montana Bureau of Mines and Geology, Special Publication* (82): 1- 9.

Reynolds, P.H., J.W. Sears. 1989. Pre- middle Eocene high- level gravel in the Garnet Range, west- central Montana. *Abstracts with Programs - Geological Society of America* 21 (5): 133.

Rotegard, L. 2006. *Annual Report – Grant- Kohrs Ranch National Historic Site, FY05.* Department of the Interior, National Park Service.

Rueger, B. F. 1996. *Palynology and its relationship to climatically induced depositional cycles in the Middle Pennsylvanian (Desmoinesian) Paradox Formation of Southeastern Utah.* U.S. Geological Survey, Bulletin: 2000- K.

Schlumberger. 2007. *Oil Field Glossary – Precipitate.* http://www.glossary.oilfield.slb.com/Display.cfm?Term=precipitate (accessed January 21, 2007).

Smith, D.J., J.H. Lambing, D.A. Nimick, C. Parrett, M. Ramey, W. Schafer, W. 1998. *Geomorphology, flood- plain tailings, and metal transport in the upper Clark Fork valley, Montana.* U. S. Geological Survey, Water- Resources Investigations: WRI 98- 4170.

Swanson, B.J. 2002. *Bank erosion and metal loading in a contaminated floodplain system, upper Clark Fork River valley, Montana.* Master's thesis: University of Montana.

Trexler, B.D.Jr., D.A. Ralston, D.A. Reece, R.E. Williams. 1975. *Sources and causes of acid mine drainage.* Idaho Bureau of Mines and Geology: Pamphlet 165.

Vogel, T.A., F.W. Cambray, L. Feher, K.N. Constenius. 1997. Petrochemistry and emplacement history of the Wasatch igneous belt, central Wasatch Mountains, Utah. *Geological Society of America – Abstracts with Programs* 29 (6): A- 282.

Winston, D. 1989. Introduction to the Belt. In *Volcanism and plutonism of western North America; Volume 2, Middle Proterozoic Belt Supergroup, western Montana,* ed. Hanshaw, P.M, 1- 6. American Geophysical Union.

Winston, D. 1989b. A Sedimentologic and tectonic interpretation of the Belt Supergroup. In *Volcanism and plutonism of western North America; Volume 2, Middle Proterozoic Belt Supergroup, western Montana,* ed. Hanshaw, P.M, 1- 6. American Geophysical Union.

Winston, D., T. Lyons. 1997. Sedimentary cycles in the St. Regis, Empire and Helena Formations of the middle Proterozoic Belt Supergroup, northwestern Montana. In *Geologic guidebook to the Belt- Purcell Supergroup, Glacier National Park and vicinity, Montana and adjacent Canada; field trip guidebook for Belt symposium III,* ed. Link, P.K., 21- 51.

Appendix A: Geologic Map Graphic

The following page provides a preview or "snapshot" of the geologic map for Grant-Kohrs Ranch National Historic Site. For a poster size PDF of this map or for digital geologic map data, please see the included CD or visit the GRE publications webpage: http://www2.nature.nps.gov/geology/inventory/gre_publications.cfm

Geologic Map of Grant-Kohrs Ranch NHS

Produced by Geologic Resources Division

March 2007

Appendix B: Scoping Summary

The following excerpts are from the GRE scoping summary for Grant-Kohrs Ranch National Historic Site. The scoping meeting occurred August 19, 2002; therefore, the contact information and Web addresses referred to herein may be outdated. Please contact the Geologic Resources Division for current information.

Executive Summary

A geologic resources evaluation workshop was held for Grant-Kohrs Ranch NHS (GRKO) on August 19, 2002 to view and discuss the park's geologic resources, to address the status of geologic mapping for compiling both paper and digital maps, and to assess resource management issues and needs. Cooperators from the NPS Geologic Resources Division (GRD), NPS Grant-Kohrs Ranch NHS, and the Montana Bureau of Mines and Technology were present for the workshop.

This involved a field trip to view the geology of the Grant-Kohrs Ranch NHS area with the Montana Bureau of Mines and Geology and a scoping session to present overviews of the NPS Inventory and Monitoring (I&M) program, the Geologic Resources Division, and the on-going Geologic Resources Evaluation (GRE). Round table discussions involving geologic issues for Grant-Kohrs Ranch NHS included interpretation, the status of geologic mapping efforts, sources of available data, and action items generated from this meeting.

Because of the upstream impacts of mining in Butte, Montana, over the last 100 years, heavy metals have impacted the GRKO area negatively. On the field trip, the group was shown a deposit of arsenic that resulted from a large flood event in 1908 in stream banks flowing through the park. Considerable soil had been developed on top of the deposit in the last 94 years. Ben Bobowski is interested in expanding the existing two park quadrangles of interest (Deer Lodge and Conleys Lake) to include more quadrangles that take in the drainage basin of the surrounding area.

Geologic Mapping

Existing Geologic Maps and Publications

The bounding coordinates for each map were noted and entered into a GIS to assemble an index geologic map. Separate coverage's were developed based on scales (1:24,000, 1:100,000, etc.) available for the specific park. Numerous geologic maps at varying scales and vintages cover the area. Index maps were distributed to each workshop participant during the scoping session.

Status

At present, there are a few maps of various scales covering the GRKO area in published form. Currently the Montana Bureau of Mines and Geology are producing a geologic map of the Deer Lodge 15' quadrangle at 1:48,000 scale of the following quadrangles: Deer Lodge (one of two current GRKO quadrangles of interest); Baggs Creek, Orofino Creek,

and Sugarloaf Mountain. They showed a draft that is very near completion and is also in ArcInfo format. There is a textual document with ancillary map information and map unit descriptions as well that will accompany this. They intend to publish it as an open file report in mid-2003.

The Conleys Lake quadrangle is not currently mapped at a scale suitable for park management needs and Dick Berg is interested in doing the mapping of the entire quadrangle at 1:24,000 scale. He anticipates that he could begin the work in 2003 upon completion of the Deer Lodge 15' geologic map. They would also deliver this map to the NPS in digital format like the Deer Lodge quadrangle.

The Conley's lake quad is covered on Butte 250k and the 62.5s and 63360s, but data are quite coarse and dated and probably more refined mapping would be desired. However, there is probably good textual information on these maps that might be able to be gleaned for the current project.

Dick Berg is interested in mapping the Conleys Lake 7.5' quad in 2003 if NPS can assist financially or otherwise. MT GS would then open file it. We'll send them our template to them.

Dick Berg suggested mapping the following quadrangles to get better coverage for the drainage basin of the GRKO area: Garrison, Conleys Lake, Deer Lodge, Racetrack, Orofino Creek, Warm Springs, Orofino Mountain, Opportunity, Ramose, Butte North, Elk Park Pass, Buxton, Butte South, Homestake, Tucker Creek

As far as a geologic report for the park, GRE staff may be able to use portions of the Deer Lodge 15' map text and may also consult the 1:250,000 Butte sheet for its ancillary information.

Digital Geologic Map Coverage

The Montana Bureau of Mines has completed digitization of numerous 1:100,000 scale maps within the state of Montana. They are available to view as an index map for download from http://www.mbmg.mtech.edu. GRE staff needs to call their publication and sales office to get FTP access to the actual digital files. Karen Porter says to call Judy for digital and hardcopy and tell them we're a federal agency and they'll allow us to have them at no charge.

Miscellaneous Notes

In a brainstorming session, GRKO staff says the main geologic issues at the park are as follows:

- Ground- water movement;
- surface water movement as affected by surficial deposits and soils and how they relate to contaminant transport from upstream acid mine drainage
- Non- point source run- off and how it is affecting neighbors and the park plant communities.
- Need to Define influences of bedrock and topography on watersheds

To better understand these processes, GRKO has an in-depth environmental quality assessment done in cooperation with several universities. It is entitled "US Department of Interior Site Characterization and Natural Resource Damage Assessment Studies, Grant-Kohrs Ranch NHS and Bureau of Land Management, 2000- 2001; Clark Fork River Operable Unit of the Milltown Reservoir Sediments NPL Site; July 8, 2002"

Dan Nottingham distributed CD- ROM copies of the above to a few of the meeting attendants, including GRE staff.

Ben Bobowsky is interested in water rights in the area and needs NPS- WRD's Horizon reports. Folks to contact in Fort Collins are either Dan Kimball or Dean Tucker, who should be able to assist with both groundwater and surficial water issues.

Ed Deal says the Montana Bureau of Mines and Geology is producing Ground- water assessments for the area that should be of great benefit to GRKO as well. It was also mentioned that Tom Patton has a database on water issues for the area at the Montana Bureau of Mines and Geology.

GRKO GIS support has come from Theresa Ely's shop in the Intermountain Region GIS Support Office, but Ben Bobowsky said he is looking to hire a full- time GIS position into GRKO in the very near future.

Other Desired Data Sets for GRKO

Soils

Soils maps are also of interest to GRKO staff. Tim Connors will check with Pete Biggam (NPS- Soil Scientist) on the status of soils mapping for the area; will require more follow- up.

List of Attendees for Grant-Kohrs Ranch National Historic Site Workshop

NAME	AFFILIATION	PHONE	E- MAIL
Dick Berg	Montana Bureau of Mines and Geology		dberg@mtech.edu
Ben Bobowski	NPS- GRKO	(406)- 846- 2070	Ben_Bobowski@nps.gov
Tim Connors	NPS, Geologic Resources Division	(303) 969- 2093	Tim_Connors@nps.gov
Ed Deal	Montana Bureau of Mines and Geology		edeal@mtech.edu
Bruce Heise	NPS, Geologic Resources Division	(303) 969- 2017	Bruce_Heise@nps.gov
Greg Nottingham	NPS- GRKO	(406)- 846- 2070, ext. 29	greg_nottingham@nps.gov
Karen Porter	Montana Bureau of Mines and Geology	(406)- 496- 4327	kporter@mtech.edu

Grant-Kohrs Ranch National Historic Site
Geologic Resource Evaluation Report

Natural Resource Report NPS/NRPC/GRD/NRR—2007/004
NPS D-58, June 2007

National Park Service
Director • Mary A. Bomar

Natural Resource Stewardship and Science
Associate Director • Michael A. Soukup

Natural Resource Program Center
The Natural Resource Program Center (NRPC) is the core of the NPS Natural Resource Stewardship and Science Directorate. The Center Director is located in Fort Collins, with staff located principally in Lakewood and Fort Collins, Colorado and in Washington, D.C. The NRPC has five divisions: Air Resources Division, Biological Resource Management Division, Environmental Quality Division, Geologic Resources Division, and Water Resources Division. NRPC also includes three offices: The Office of Education and Outreach, the Office of Inventory, Monitoring and Evaluation, and the Office of Natural Resource Information Systems. In addition, Natural Resource Web Management and Partnership Coordination are cross- cutting disciplines under the Center Director. The multidisciplinary staff of NRPC is dedicated to resolving park resource management challenges originating in and outside units of the national park system.

Geologic Resources Division
Chief • David B. Shaver
Planning Evaluation and Permits Branch Chief • Carol McCoy

Credits
Author • Trista Thornberry- Ehrlich
Editing • Sid Covington and Melanie Ransmeier
Digital Map Production • Georgia Hybels, Anne Poole and Montana Bureau of Mines and Geology
Map Layout Design • Andrea Croskrey